DIRTY AND DANGEROUS JOBS

Pit Crew Worker

By Geoffrey M. Horn

Reading Consultant: Susan Nations, M.Ed.,
Author/Literacy Coach/Consultant in Literacy Development

Marshall Cavendish
Benchmark
New York

Published by Marshall Cavendish Benchmark
An imprint of Marshall Cavendish Corporation

Other Marshall Cavendish Offices:
Marshall Cavendish International (Asia) Private Limited, 1 New Industrial Road, Singapore 536196 • Marshall Cavendish International (Thailand) Co Ltd. 253 Asoke, 12th Flr, Sukhumvit 21 Road, Klongtoey Nua, Wattana, Bangkok 10110, Thailand • Marshall Cavendish (Malaysia) Sdn Bhd, Times Subang, Lot 46, Subang Hi-Tech Industrial Park, Batu Tiga, 40000 Shah Alam, Selangor Darul Ehsan, Malaysia

Marshall Cavendish is a trademark of Times Publishing Limited

Library of Congress Cataloging-in-Publication Data
Horn, Geoffrey M.
       Pit crew worker / by Geoffrey M. Horn.
              p. cm. — (Dirty and dangerous jobs)
       Includes index.
       ISBN 978-1-60870-177-3
       1. Automobile racing—Juvenile literature.
       2. Pit crews—Juvenile literature. I. Title.
   GV1029.H58 2011
   796.72—dc22   2010000210

Developed for Marshall Cavendish Benchmark by RJF Publishing LLC (www.RJFpublishing.com)
Editor: Amanda Hudson
Design: Westgraphix LLC/Tammy West
Photo Research: Edward A. Thomas
Map Illustrator: Stefan Chabluk
Index: Nila Glikin

Cover: Marco Andretti makes a pit stop on May 27, 2007, at the Indianapolis 500.

The photographs in this book are used by permission and through the courtesy of: Cover, 6, 8, 10, 15, 18, 20: Getty Images; 4, 14, 28: AP Images; 11: Bloomberg/Getty Images; 12: AFP/Getty Images; 16, 22, 23, 24, 25: Getty Images for NASCAR; 17: Sports Illustrated/Getty Images; 27: © Thomas R. Fletcher/Alamy.

Printed in Malaysia (T).
135642

CONTENTS

Words defined in the glossary are in **bold** type
the first time they appear in the text.

It's the Pits!

Driving the car on the left, Al Unser Jr. won the Indianapolis 500 in the closest victory in the history of the race.

On a chilly, windy morning in late May 1992, 33 race cars began circling a track in Indianapolis, Indiana. Three hours, 43 minutes, and 5.148 seconds later, the winning car—driven by Al Unser Jr.—completed its 200th and final **lap**. According to the official clock, Unser beat the second-place car by 0.043 seconds. His victory margin, less than one-tenth of a second, was the slimmest in the history of the Indianapolis 500.

Unser needed all his talents to win his narrow victory. He also needed the finely tuned skills of a top-notch pit crew. Whenever his car had to stop, the crew worked as fast as possible to get his car ready to run again. The pit crew filled the fuel tank, changed the tires, and got him back out on the track—all in less time than it takes most people to read this sentence.

Building a Team

Al Unser's uncle was Bobby Unser, who was also a famous race car driver. Bobby was one of the top drivers of his time. He won the Indy 500 three times—in 1968, 1975, and 1981. His crew set an Indy 500 record in 1976 for the fastest pit stop: 4 seconds. Bobby knew that although top drivers get most of the money and glory, auto racing is truly a team sport.

"At 220 miles [355 kilometers] per hour, there's no such thing as a small job," Bobby wrote. "If one adjustment is not right, one detail left undone, the car could hit a wall, crash, and erupt into a ball of flame. There may be one person driving the car, but there are a lot of people who make a car go fast, keep it together, and help make it win. Putting together the right team—pit crew, mechanics, sponsors, and engineers—takes a long time."

The Indianapolis 500

The Indianapolis 500 is one of the most important auto races in the United States. This race takes place each year on a track called the Indianapolis Motor Speedway. Because the speedway was originally built from bricks, the track is often called the Brickyard. Today, however, the track has been repaved, and only a few bricks remain. Cars must drive around the 2.5-mile (4-kilometer) track 200 times to complete the 500-mile (800-kilometer) race.

Bobby Unser gets fuel during a race on July 4, 1970. His crew set an Indy 500 record in 1976 for fastest pit stop.

Taking a Beating

High-speed racing is rough on race cars. **Indycars**—the cars that race at the Indy 500—have more than four times the power of a regular car. They must go from 0 to 100 miles (160 kilometers) per hour in less than three seconds. When an Indy driver enters a turn at full speed, the forces on the car equal those felt by astronauts in a space shuttle when it takes off.

In the practice rounds for the 2009 race, speeds topped 225 miles (360 kilometers) an hour. At speeds like these, fuel burns rapidly. Tires wear out quickly. Parts shake loose or break down. Trips to the pit are a must.

On the Pit Road

When a race car needs to make a pit stop, it pulls off the inside of the track and onto the pit road (also called the pit lane). Each car has its own service area, which is called a **pit stall**, or pit box. Along the pit road is a wall that separates the service areas from the infield, which is the area within the oval track. Members of the pit crew work directly on the vehicle. Other members of the race team work behind the wall. These members pass tires, hoses, and other equipment over the wall to the pit crew. They do not enter the pit stall.

The race team is led by a crew chief. The crew chief puts the crew together and oversees every part of its performance. Jeff Hammond, a **NASCAR** crew chief, compares his crew to a perfectly trained dance team. "Jack the car, pop the **lug nuts**, mount the tire, tighten the nuts, drop the car, go around the car, and do it all again. Go, go, go. Keep moving and get that car out of there and back on the track."

Part of the Crew

Champion pit crew chief Jeff Hammond started out as a tire changer in 1974. In his book *Real Men Work in the Pits*, he talks about how he chose his career.

"When I was 15 or 16 years old . . . I realized that I was pretty good at working on cars and that I loved doing it and what I really wanted to do was be part of a pit crew. I wanted to be one of the guys jumping over the wall and changing tires or working the jack. That, to me, was really exciting."

7

Speed Read: A Quick Look at Indycar Racing

Built long and low to the ground, Indycars have a single seat, and an open **cockpit** where the driver sits. They are called **open-wheel cars** because the wheels are outside the main body of the vehicle. (On a standard car, the wheels sit beneath the body.)

Indycars are named for the Indianapolis 500 race, which began in 1911. Today, Indycar drivers compete in the Indy Racing League. The season includes the Indy 500 along with other events in the United States and overseas.

Indycars have a single seat and an open cockpit for the driver.

Speed Is Money

Life on a pit crew is greasy, grimy, and often dangerous work. Crew members can—and do—get hurt in the pits. Sloppy work costs time and money. Carelessness can cost lives.

What kind of person is cut out for life on a pit crew? For someone who loves working on cars, this just might be a dream job. Many pit crew workers were "car crazy" from a young age. They watched auto racing on TV, went to the racetrack as often as they could, and learned the names of the top drivers and race teams. They helped family members work on their cars and took car repair courses in high school. They learned everything they could about cars, inside and out.

The job requires more than just loving cars, however. Working on a pit crew means working well with others and joining a team. During the week, many pit crew members also work on race cars at the team garage. They exercise with strength and conditioning coaches to keep themselves in great shape.

Indycar Pit Crew

Indycar racing rules allow six crew members to work directly on the car. Four of the six are tire changers. The fifth crew member operates the **airjack**, a device that uses compressed air to lift the car off the ground. The sixth crew member fuels the car and uses a vent hose to clean up spilled fuel.

Other crew members stand on the other side of the wall. Their job is to help the six members in the pit stall. They extend fuel and air hoses over the wall, pass tires to the tire changers, and spray water on the car to wash away any spilled fuel.

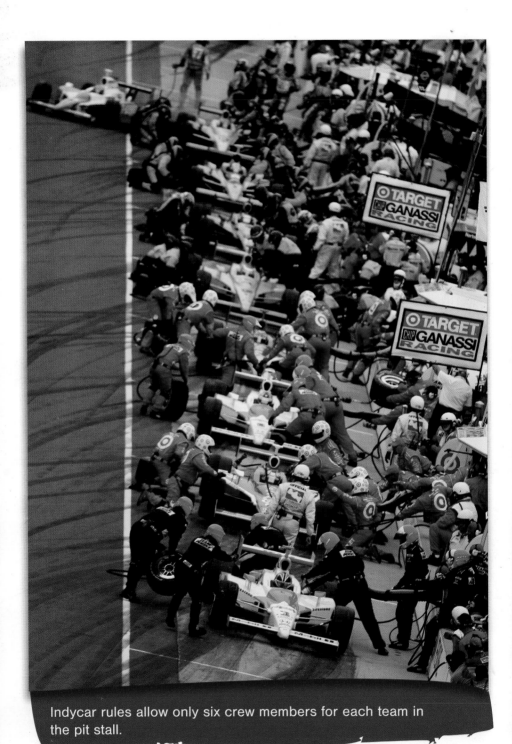

Indycar rules allow only six crew members for each team in the pit stall.

Crew members review their races and team practices on video to see how they can improve. They know that every tenth of a second they can cut from a pit stop may mean many thousands of dollars in prize money. The most successful crews earn the highest pay. Winning crews get bonuses, which can quickly add up.

Join a Pit Crew, See the World

Pit crews travel where the action is. Although most Indycar races are run in the United States, the sport is popular in many other countries. In recent years, major Indycar races have been held in Canada, Brazil, and Japan. One of Japan's leading tracks is the Twin Ring Motegi, which is located in the town of Motegi. Danica Patrick made history at Motegi in April 2008 when she became the first woman ever to win an Indycar race. She gave a lot of the credit for her win to pit crew member Kyle Moyer, who found ways to help her save fuel and time.

In April 2008, Danica Patrick became the first woman to win an Indycar race.

Caution Flags

Sarah Fisher raced in the Indianapolis 500 when she was only 19 years old.

Sarah Fisher has been driving Indycars since 1999. In 2000, at the age of 19, she became the youngest woman to race in the Indianapolis 500. Today, she is a full-time driver and team owner. Her co-owner and team manager is her husband, Andy O'Gara.

O'Gara was one of Fisher's tire changers. On a national TV show she described how she "ran over him" while making a pit stop in 2003. "I just gave him a little nudge," she said. The two began dating, and they were married in 2007.

Pit Hazards

Most pit road accidents do not have such happy endings. One of the worst accidents in the history of NASCAR racing took place on the pit lane at Atlanta Motor Speedway in November 1990. As NASCAR driver Ricky Rudd rushed into the pit lane, he lost control of his car. It slammed into Bill Elliott's vehicle, which had stopped for a tire change. Elliott's rear tire changer, Mike Rich, was killed in the wreck, and two of Elliott's other pit crew workers were injured.

Out-of-control cars are not the only hazard. Pit crew workers who jack up cars and change tires also risk burned hands, jammed fingers, strained muscles, and bashed knees. Fire is another major danger. In July 2009, Indycar driver Tony Kanaan suffered burns on his face and hands when a fuel hose broke in the pit lane at a track in Edmonton, in Alberta, Canada.

Markus Burger, who refuels cars for a **Formula One** racing team, recalls an accident that happened when a car tried to speed out of the pits while its fuel hose was still attached. Fuel shot out of the hose and burst into flames. "It was certainly a bit heated!" he said.

Stock Cars and Indycars

NASCAR stands for National Association for Stock Car Auto Racing. Unlike Indycars, which are long and low, **stock cars** are shaped like standard cars. Another difference is that the driver of a stock car sits in a closed cockpit, while the cockpit of an Indycar is open. In a stock car, the wheels sit beneath the car's body, as they do on a standard car.

NASCAR crew members push Jeff Burton's car as flames shoot out from an engine fire.

Safety First

Groups that sponsor races take safety seriously. In NASCAR races, for example, the speed limit on the pit road is usually 55 miles (90 kilometers) per hour or less. Cars get penalties if they pit outside the box. This means the nose of the car must be inside the front line of the box, and the rear must not extend beyond the back line. To avoid getting hit by other cars, crew members cannot jump off the wall and into the pit stall until their car is just about to enter the stall.

NASCAR also requires crew members to wear approved safety gear. All crew members who enter the pit box must wear helmets and gloves for protection. Their suits

Speed Read: A Quick Look at NASCAR

Stock-car racing has changed a great deal since NASCAR held its first race at Daytona, Florida, in 1948. At first, NASCAR race cars actually were based on standard passenger cars. By the late 1960s, however, all NASCAR vehicles were specially built for speed and safety. It costs a lot of money to make and maintain a NASCAR vehicle. Major companies supply the funds. In return, they get to put their company names in large letters on the race car.

NASCAR races more than stock cars. Since 1995, NASCAR has also run a truck racing series. In 2009 there were a total of more than 1,200 NASCAR races at about 100 tracks in the United States.

Major companies help pay to maintain NASCAR vehicles.

Teams are penalized if their car is not completely inside the pit box.

and shoes—even their underwear—must be made from materials that do not burn easily.

Despite these rules, accidents can happen. Crew members must be quick on their feet to get out of harm's way. "Anything can happen on [a] pit road," notes Mark Morrison, a strength and conditioning coach for Hendrick Motorsports, near Charlotte, North Carolina. "Quick reaction time, like in any professional sport, is key."

Hit on the Heels

NASCAR **jackman** Shaun Peet works in the pit on the Number 83 Toyota driven by Brian Vickers. "I've joked that being a jackman is a cakewalk," he said in 2008. "But the reality is it's very dangerous. . . . I've been very fortunate that I've never been blasted by a car, but I've been grazed a couple times and had my heels run over. . . . I live to ride on the edge. I'm more scared of being bored than anything else. If you focus on the fear, then you're not cut out for this job."

NASCAR Pit Crew

In NASCAR auto races, seven crew members are allowed over the wall at most pit stops. First, the jackman uses a powered jack to lift the car wheels off the ground. Next, two crew members—the front and rear tire changers—remove the worn-out tire and the wheel on which it is mounted. They do this by using an air-powered tool that loosens the five lug nuts that connect the wheel to the car.

Two other crew members—the front and rear tire carriers—bring the fresh tires and wheels to the changers. The changers place the new wheels in position and tighten the five lug nuts to hold them in place. Meanwhile, the "gas man" fuels the car, and the "catch can man" holds a can to collect any gas that may spill. At some spots, officials may allow an eighth crew member over the wall to clean the car's windshield. Other crew members stand behind the wall to help the workers in the pit box.

A jackman practices at a garage in Statesville, North Carolina.

17

Need for Speed

Helio Castroneves won an Indycar race in 2009 with a 6-second pit stop.

Refuel the car. Loosen the lug nuts. Take off the old tires. Put on the new tires. Tighten the lug nuts. Clean the windshield. In the 1990s, champion NASCAR teams might have finished all these tasks in a 16-second pit stop. Today, 14 seconds is routine. Winning teams do it in 13 seconds or less.

In other types of auto races, the pit stops are even faster. For example, at the Texas Motor Speedway in June 2009, Helio Castroneves won his Indycar race with a pit stop of only 6 seconds.

Working Against Time

Fast times require hard work. Team members work out at the gym and practice in the pits. A stopwatch is one of a pit crew's most important tools.

"After every pit stop practice we have times from all guys and all the jobs," says Gerard Lecoq, chief mechanic for Toyota's Formula One racing team. "We have them on a chart and put it on the wall so there is a kind of competition. The guys on one tire see they are slower than another, and next time they try even harder to do it faster. . . . Then they exchange tips, and this is how we improve—you can see the progression during the season."

Pit Strategy

Racing teams need more than quick pit times. They also need a winning pit **strategy**. A key decision is how much fuel to give the car. In Formula One (F1) racing, a pit stop typically takes between 6 and 11 seconds, depending on how much fuel the car receives.

Formula One Pit Crew

Up to 25 crew members may be involved in a single pit stop. The process begins when the "lollipop man" lowers a lollipop-shaped sign to guide the driver into the pit. Two crew members—one at the front, the other at the rear—jack up the car. Eight crew members (two for each wheel) change the tires and loosen and then tighten the lug nuts that hold the wheels in place. Two additional pit crew members refuel the car. While all this happens, other crew members handle repairs and stand by with fire safety equipment. When all repairs have been done, the lollipop man raises the sign, and the driver pulls out of the pit.

Speed Read: A Quick Look at Formula One

Like Indycars, Formula One (F1) race cars have open wheels and an open cockpit. F1 cars are lighter than Indycars (and much lighter than stock cars) but just as powerful. F1 races feature many sharp twists and turns. The cars are designed to make quick changes of speed and direction.

Unlike NASCAR and Indycar racing, which began in the United States, Formula One racing started in Europe. Many F1 races use the term Grand Prix (pronounced *GRAHN PREE*), which is French for "Grand Prize." The first Grand Prix race was held in France in 1901. F1 racing officially began in 1950. F1 drivers compete all over the world, with races in Europe, Asia, and South America.

Formula One (F1) racing officially began in 1950, when this photo was taken.

An F1 engine can usually go between 2.8 and 3.3 miles on a gallon of fuel (from 1.2 to 1.4 kilometers per liter). Fuel is heavy. In a 300-kilometer (186-mile) race, the total amount of fuel used by an F1 car adds up to nearly one-third the weight of the car!

In F1 racing, a racing team can choose how many pit stops to make. Suppose the car makes very few pit stops. This saves pit time, but the heavy weight of the fuel after a fill-up makes the car run more slowly. Now, suppose the car makes many pit stops. It spends more time in the pit but because the car is carrying less fuel weight, it runs faster on the track. Which strategy will work best in a particular race? That depends on many factors, including track conditions, the speed of the car—and the speed of the pit crew.

Avoiding Costly Mistakes

Even while working at top speed, drivers and crew members must be careful to avoid mistakes on pit roads. Top teams can—and do—lose races because of pit errors. When they make too many mistakes, team members lose their jobs.

In NASCAR racing, for example, one of the biggest stars and most successful drivers is Dale Earnhardt Jr. By the end of the 2008 season, Earnhardt had earned more than $45 million on the racetrack. In 2009, however, his team had a series of embarrassing pit mishaps. In February, at the Daytona 500 in Florida, Earnhardt mistakenly drove past his pit stall. Later in the same race, he got a penalty for pitting outside the box.

In April, in the Samsung 500 at the Texas Motor Speedway, Earnhardt's front tire changer forgot to replace

Dale Earnhardt Jr. shares a laugh with a pit crew member as he is helped into his car.

a lug nut on the left front wheel. A lug nut error two weeks later at the Subway Fresh Fit 500 in Phoenix, Arizona, resulted in another penalty. Earnhardt's crew chief—his cousin, Tony Eury Jr.—was replaced in May.

Pit Crew Contests

Pit teams test their skills in the pits on race day. In addition, they can test their speed in special pit crew competitions. In NASCAR's yearly Pit Crew Challenge, top teams compete against each other. Each team must refuel its car, change the tires, and then push the car 40 yards (37 meters). Teams get penalties for mistakes, such as spilling too much fuel or leaving too much fuel in the can. In Indycar racing, events at the Indianapolis 500 also include a pit crew challenge.

NASCAR holds the Pit Crew Challenge every year for teams to test their skills.

Many pit crew workers are drawn to the job because they love cars.

Pit crew members come from many different backgrounds. Some dreamed of becoming race car drivers but later changed their minds. Jeff Hammond, who became a NASCAR crew chief, wanted to drive, but his mother said no. "She didn't want me to drive, and I had to respect that," he wrote later.

Nicole Addison, who worked with a NASCAR crew as a rear tire changer, has always loved cars and competition. "I like to get dirty and work on the car itself," she told a reporter. "It became my passion in high school and I just wanted to be around anything to do with racing."

Women in the Pits

The number of women who work in pit crews is small but growing. Lisa Smokstad began working as a tire changer in NASCAR races in 1999. NASCAR truck race driver Shawna Robinson worked with an all-female pit crew for part of the 2003 racing season. Nicole Addison got her first pit job in NASCAR truck racing as a tire changer with Express MotorSports in 2005.

Lisa Smokstad has worked in a NASCAR pit crew since 1999.

Full-Time or Part-Time?

For some pit crew members, race day is part of a full-time commitment to auto racing. For example, nearly all crew members employed by Hendrick Motorsports have full-time jobs designing, building, and repairing cars in the team shop. More than 500 people work for the company, which has its own gym. During the racing season, pit crew members exercise in the gym four days a week. Hendrick teams also run pit practices two or three times a week.

Members of crews sponsored by other companies may spend the week in non-racing jobs. For example, the United Parcel Service (UPS) sponsors a NASCAR racing team based in Charlotte, North Carolina. UPS pit crew members have held day jobs as truck drivers, firefighters, auto dealers, and farmers.

Pit Stop Athletes

Whatever day job they hold, all pit crew members must be good athletes. They have to be strong. In a NASCAR pit stop, the "gas man" raises a 12-gallon (45-liter) fuel can that weighs 80 pounds (36 kilograms). A wheel and tire weigh 64 pounds (29 kilograms), and the jack weighs 38 pounds (17 kilograms). It takes a great deal of strength to move quickly and safely with such heavy and bulky equipment. Tire changers "have to have really good hand-eye coordination and hand speed," says crew chief Alan Gustafson.

In recent years, racing teams have looked for pit crew members who were standouts in other sports. For example, NASCAR jackman Shaun Peet played ice hockey in college and also played with a minor-league pro team. Peet was

Pit Crew Courses

Several schools offer pit crew training. One of the best known schools is Performance Instruction & Training (PIT) in Mooresville, North Carolina. PIT runs an eight-week "Pit Crew U" program. Another pit crew training program is Crewschool, which is based in Asheboro, North Carolina. Crewschool offers a 14-week, hands-on course for people who want to pursue a career in stock car racing.

Members of "Pit Crew U" practice a drill in Mooresville, North Carolina.

Alan Gustafson, shown here holding his son, is a NASCAR crew chief.

raised in Canada, where his father owned a garage and an auto-parts store. "Growing up, I was on the ice practicing," he says. "But I was also in the garage turning wrenches, so it has come pretty easy for me."

Tire carrier Dion Williams was a college linebacker with Wake Forest and played one season in the National Football League with the Minnesota Vikings.

Williams says being a member of a pit crew in a top racing event is actually "more competitive than football. . . . With a pit crew, you can't make any mistakes. It's about who can do it under pressure."

So You Want to Be a Pit Crew Worker

Is pit crew worker the right job for you? Consider these key questions:

- **Do you love cars?**

  Most pit crew members get their start working on cars at home. You'll want to learn all you can about race cars and race car drivers. You won't need a college degree, but taking a pit crew training course can help.

- **Do you like getting your hands dirty?**

  Working in the pits and building and repairing race cars at the garage can be greasy, grimy work.

- **Are you in good physical condition?**

  Pit crews work with heavy and bulky equipment. Top teams work hard and train hard.

- **Are you safety-conscious?**

  You need to be quick in the pits, but you also need to be careful. Sloppy work can lose races and end careers.

- **Can you handle the pressure?**

  A fraction of a second in the pit can mean the difference between a win and a loss. Winning teams earn big bonuses.

GLOSSARY

airjack: A device that uses compressed air to lift a car off the ground at a pit stop, so the tires can be changed.

cockpit: In a race car, the area where the driver sits.

Formula One: A type of auto racing developed in Europe. It involves lightweight but powerful open-wheel vehicles with open cockpits. The vehicles race on tracks that have many sharp turns.

Indycar: A race car with open wheels and an open cockpit, named for the type of cars that compete in the annual Indianapolis (Indy) 500.

jackman: A pit crew member who uses a powered jack to lift the race car off the ground so the tires can be replaced.

lap: In auto racing, one full circuit around a racetrack. For example, if a race is 500 miles (800 kilometers) long, and one lap around the track covers a distance of 2.5 miles (4 kilometers), then the race consists of 200 laps around the track.

lug nut: Metal fasteners that are used to attach a wheel onto a car.

NASCAR: Stands for National Association for Stock Car Auto Racing, the major organization sponsoring stock-car racing in the United States.

open-wheel car: A race car in which the wheels sit outside the main body of the vehicle. Examples of open-wheel cars include Indycars and Formula One cars.

pit stall: On a pit road, the assigned place where the pit crew services a race car; also known as the pit box.

stock car: A race car with a closed cockpit and wheels sitting under the vehicle's body, designed to look like a standard passenger car.

strategy: In auto racing, a plan designed to give the driver the best possible chance of winning.

BOOKS

Gifford, Clive. *Racing: The Ultimate Motorsports Encyclopedia*. Boston: Kingfisher, 2006.

Kelley, K. C. *NASCAR*. New York: Marshall Cavendish Benchmark, 2010.

Mattern, Joanne. *Behind Every Great Driver: Stock Car Teams*. New York: Children's Press, 2007.

Mello, Tara Baukus. *The Pit Crew*. New York: Chelsea House, 2007.

Schaefer, A. R. *Racing with the Pit Crew*. Mankato, MN: Capstone Press, 2005.

Stewart, Mark, and Mike Kennedy. *NASCAR in the Pits*. Minneapolis: Lerner, 2008.

WEBSITES

http://www.formula1.com
Follow all the twists and turns of some of the world's most challenging racetracks.

http://www.indycar.com
This official Indycar site takes you behind the wheel with all the top drivers and major races.

http://www.nascar.com
Official NASCAR videos let you share the speed and excitement of one of the most popular sports in the United States.

About the Author Geoffrey M. Horn has written more than four dozen books for young people and adults, along with hundreds of articles for encyclopedias and other works. He lives in southwestern Virginia, in the foothills of the Blue Ridge Mountains, with his wife and five cats. He dedicates this book to the memory of Maggie and Una.